WEST HIGHLAND

A BOOK OF 21 POSTCARDS

S0-AWW-641

BROWNTROUT PUBLISHERS
SAN FRANCISCO • CALIFORNIA

BROWNTROUT PUBLISHERS

P. O. BOX 280070 • SAN FRANCISCO • CALIFORNIA 94128-0070
800 777 7812 • www.browntrout.com

ISBN: 1-56313-921-9
TITLE: 921

BROWNTROUT publishes a large line of calendars, photographic books, and postcard books.
Please write for more information.

Printed in Hong Kong

WEST HIGHLAND TERRIERS

"The great pleasure of a dog is that you may make a fool of yourself with him and not only will he not scold you, but he will make a fool of himself too."
— SAMUEL BUTLER

BROWNTROUT PUBLISHERS • SAN FRANCISCO, CALIFORNIA

WEST HIGHLAND TERRIERS

"The poor dog, in life the firmest friend /
The first to welcome, foremost to defend."
—LORD BYRON

PUBLISHED BY BROWNTROUT • SAN FRANCISCO, CALIFORNIA

WEST HIGHLAND TERRIERS

"They are better than human beings, because they know but do not tell."

—EMILY DICKINSON

PUBLISHED BY BROWNTROUT • SAN FRANCISCO, CALIFORNIA

WEST HIGHLAND TERRIERS

"…he will be our friend for always and always and always."
—Rudyard Kipling

PUBLISHED BY BROWNTROUT • SAN FRANCISCO, CALIFORNIA

WEST HIGHLAND TERRIERS

" 'Tis sweet to know there is an eye will mark /
Our coming and look brighter when we come." —LORD BYRON

PUBLISHED BY BROWNTROUT • SAN FRANCISCO, CALIFORNIA

WEST HIGHLAND TERRIERS

"Loving friend, the gift of one / Who her own true faith has run
Through thy lower nature, / Be my benediction said
With my hand upon thy head, / Gentle fellow-creature!"
—ELIZABETH BARRETT BROWNING

PUBLISHED BY BROWNTROUT • SAN FRANCISCO, CALIFORNIA

PHOTOGRAPHY ©1998 JERRY SHULMAN

WEST HIGHLAND TERRIERS

"The dog represents all that is best in man." —ÉTIENNE CHARLET

PUBLISHED BY BROWNTROUT • SAN FRANCISCO, CALIFORNIA

WEST HIGHLAND TERRIERS

"Don't keep your dog always on a leash
if you want him to be attached to you." —A. WILLEMETZ

PUBLISHED BY BROWNTROUT • SAN FRANCISCO, CALIFORNIA

WEST HIGHLAND TERRIERS

"A dog will never forget the crumb thou gavest him." —SA'DI

PUBLISHED BY BROWNTROUT • SAN FRANCISCO, CALIFORNIA

WEST HIGHLAND TERRIERS

"I would rather see a portrait of a dog that I know,
than all the allegorical paintings in the world."   —SAMUEL JOHNSON

PUBLISHED BY BROWNTROUT • SAN FRANCISCO, CALIFORNIA

WEST HIGHLAND TERRIERS

"A good dog deserves a good bone." —BEN JOHNSON

PUBLISHED BY BROWNTROUT • SAN FRANCISCO, CALIFORNIA

WEST HIGHLAND TERRIERS

"Histories are more full of examples of fidelity of dogs than of friends."
— ALEXANDER POPE

PUBLISHED BY BROWNTROUT • SAN FRANCISCO, CALIFORNIA

WEST HIGHLAND TERRIERS

"Here, gentlemen, a dog teaches us a lesson in humanity."
—NAPOLEON BONAPARTE

PUBLISHED BY BROWNTROUT • SAN FRANCISCO, CALIFORNIA

WEST HIGHLAND TERRIERS

"I agree with Agassiz that dogs possess something very like a conscience."
— CHARLES DARWIN

PUBLISHED BY BROWNTROUT • SAN FRANCISCO, CALIFORNIA

WEST HIGHLAND TERRIERS

"The Almighty, who gave the dog to be the companion of our pleasures and toils, hath invested him with a nature noble and incapable of deceipt."

—Sir Walter Scott

PUBLISHED BY BROWNTROUT • SAN FRANCISCO, CALIFORNIA

WEST HIGHLAND TERRIERS

"The more I see of men, the more I admire dogs." — MADAME DE SÉVIGNÉ

PUBLISHED BY BROWNTROUT • SAN FRANCISCO, CALIFORNIA

WEST HIGHLAND TERRIERS

"Dogs are indeed the most affectionate,
and amiable animals of the whole brute creation." —EDMUND BURKE

PUBLISHED BY BROWNTROUT • SAN FRANCISCO, CALIFORNIA

WEST HIGHLAND TERRIERS

"In the concurring opinion of the wise, a dog, thankful for his food,
is more worthy than a human being who is devoid of gratitude."   —SA'DI

PUBLISHED BY BROWNTROUT • SAN FRANCISCO, CALIFORNIA

WEST HIGHLAND TERRIERS

"Dog. A kind of additional or subsidiary deity designed
to catch the overflow and surplus of the world's worship."

—AMBROSE BIERCE

PUBLISHED BY BROWNTROUT • SAN FRANCISCO, CALIFORNIA

WEST HIGHLAND TERRIERS

"Qui me amat, amat et canum meum." —St. Bernard

PUBLISHED BY BROWNTROUT • SAN FRANCISCO, CALIFORNIA

WEST HIGHLAND TERRIERS

"The dog was created specially for children. He is the god of frolic."
—HENRY WARD BEECHER

PUBLISHED BY BROWNTROUT • SAN FRANCISCO, CALIFORNIA